# Thai Takeout Recipe Book

*Start Cooking Thai Food Recipes Inspired by Your Favorite Takeout (2022 Guide for Beginners)*

## Chuan Ahunai

# TABLE OF CONTENTS

# INTRODUCTION

Thai food has its own distinct personality. It's easy to tell it apart from Chinese and other Asian cuisines. Thai cuisine has its distinct blend of sweet, sour, salty, bitter, and spicy flavors. Popular Thai takeaway meals as we know them, however, may no longer be regarded as genuine by purists, as with any takeout recipes. Thai takeaway foods are typically westernized (yet tasty) approximations of their traditional counterparts. This recipe book will assist you in preparing your favorite foods at home. Most are simple to prepare without sacrificing the takeaway flavor. Cooking at home may require some effort, but it is always healthier and more enjoyable.

# HISTORY

Thai cuisine is the consequence of East and West colliding. It is claimed to be mostly Chinese, but with various touches — ingredients and cooking techniques — from nearby Asian civilizations as well as distant cultures from Europe that give it its own distinct taste. Europeans were thought to have introduced chilies, whereas Indians brought curries to them. Thai cuisine is also reported to have been inspired by Arabs, Persians, Burmese, Laotians, and Khmers. Thais experimented with their own resources, reducing the spiciness with their own herbs and replacing items like ghee with coconut oil and cow's milk with coconut milk. Thai cuisine has different features depending on where it comes from. The northern areas, for example, are greatly impacted by China, whilst the southern parts are heavily influenced by Malay. Thai food as we know it in the West is thought to be evocative of central Thailand's historic royal cuisine of the former Ayutthaya Kingdom. The numerous civilizations that have contributed to Thailand's vivid and fascinating tastes are unmistakably Thai. Thailand was never colonized, hence it was able to retain its unique culture and food. When the monarchy was deposed in the 1940s, Thailand's first Prime Minister, Phibun, launched a campaign to strengthen the country's cultural identity. Foreign food was prohibited from being sold or consumed. Chinese street cuisine was outlawed, and a call was issued for the development of a meal that they could name their own. This resulted in the development of Pad Thai (or Phat Thai), their national dish. Thai restaurants are now judged on how effectively they cook Pad Thai.

Asian takeaway in the United States started in the 1900s, mostly with Chinese immigration, while Thai takeouts did not appear until much later. There may have been a limited number of Thai restaurants constructed between the late 1950s and the late 1960s, but takeouts seem to have started to proliferate in the 1970s. Traditionalists see Thai takeaway in the West as overly westernized. Thai restaurants in the West may also be limited by the population's taste buds as well as the availability of ingredients. Whereas real Thai food is distinguished by its robust tastes, westernized Thai pales in contrast. Westernized Thai

4

recipes include greater and larger-sized quantities of meat and fewer herbs. Dried shrimp, a staple of authentic Thai cuisine, may be hard to get in the West. Perhaps it is seen as too eccentric for western taste. Regardless, many people are growing more experimental and appreciative of original tastes. Meanwhile, with the inflow of Western visitors to Thailand, Thai cooks are increasingly creating many more western-inspired and fusion cuisines.

## Thai Cuisine Ingredients

Thailand has infused its ingredients into recipes brought to them by outsiders such as the Chinese and Indians. The following items are often found in their dishes.

Black peppercorns are utilized in a variety of foods and were the initial source of heat in Thai cookery. Chilies were not discovered until the 16th century.

## Chipotle Oil

This deep crimson oil, known as nam phrik show, is nearly always present in Thai cuisine and is easier to utilize than fresh chilies. It may be kept in the refrigerator and used whenever it is required.

Thai or Bird chilies are used in stir-fries and sauces. Cayenne peppers are the most often used in curries. Dried chilies are also used to produce curry paste, as well as in stir-fries and soups. Chilies may cause pepper burn and skin irritation, so wear rubber gloves while handling them and avoid getting them in your eyes. When cooking, avoid inhaling their powder or fumes since this might irritate the respiratory tract.

Cilantro (Pak Chee) is a common garnish in Thai cookery that employs the plant's leaves, stems, and roots. It is a fragrant plant with a somewhat lemony taste. Some people describe its taste as "soapy." Because heat destroys its taste, it is normally used raw as a garnish. Thais regard this plant for its therapeutic benefits as well. It is supposed to help digestion and aid in the clearance of toxins from the body. It's

5

also known as Chinese parsley or coriander, however, we'll use the name coriander to refer to the plant's seed.

Dairy may not be as popular, thus coconut milk is utilized instead. Coconut milk from a can may also be utilized.

## Curry Powder

This is a key component in Thai curries, giving them a unique taste. Red curry paste, green curry paste, yellow curry paste, Panang curry paste, and Massaman curry paste are all available. Each is made up of a unique blend of herbs and spices to give it a distinct taste. These are also available ready-made at Asian supermarkets.

## Shrimp, Dried

Kung haeng is used to enhance the umami flavor in Thai meals. It is used in the preparation of chili and curry pastes. It may also be found in Pad Thai and Thai salads.

## Sauce de Poisson

It is produced from fermented fish (typically anchovies) in brine and is known as nam pla. To enhance salinity and taste, most Thai foods employ fish sauce rather than soy sauce. Vietnamese and Filipino variants are also available, however, they differ in taste and saltiness.

## Galangal

This has a similar appearance to ginger but is lighter in color with pink undertones. It has a particular taste, and it is finest when fresh. If using dried galangal, soak it first until softened. For every 1 part fresh needed in the recipe, use 2 parts powder.

## Herbs

Fresh herbs like cilantro, mint, Thai basil, and Vietnamese coriander are common in Thai cuisine.

## Lemongrass

It has a lemony taste with a dash of ginger and is also known as takraii. It may also be used dry, as a powder, or as a paste. When used fresh to form a paste, pounding or bruising using a mortar and pestle is supposed to improve flavor release.


Lime limes are used in Thai cooking to provide zest and sourness. Lime is used to provide acidity and perfume to soups and curries. It also has a meat tenderizing effect.

**Noodles**
Thais consume a wide variety of noodles. Here are a few examples:
*Banana Noodles (Wun Sen)
Transparent noodles, glass noodles, cellophane noodles, and thread noodles are other names for bean noodles or mung bean noodles. Depending on the recipe, these noodles may be cooked and prepared in a variety of ways. When immersed in hot water, they become malleable, and when cooked, they become transparent.

- Noodles made with wide rice (Sen Han)
    Large rice noodles are often used in stir-fries. Drunken Noodles (Pad Kee Mow) and Stir-Fried Soy Sauce Noodles are popular dishes (Pad See Ew).

- Rice Sticks/Medium Rice Noodles (Sen Lek)
The noodles are used in Pad Thai. They are almost the same size and shape as linguine.

- Thin Rice Noodles/Rice Sticks (Sen Yai)
Thinnest, flattest rice noodles are used in soups and stir fry.

- Rice Vermicelli (Sen Mee) is the thinnest round rice noodle that may be confused with bean noodles. They must also be soaked in water before adding to recipes, and when cooked, they become white.

Palm sugar is a sweetener derived from the sap of the palmyra palm. Flex the tubs if you purchase them in tubs to check for suppleness. If it's too firm, reheat it in the microwave for a few seconds

7

to soften it. You may make a powder out of it by pounding or grating it, or you can soften it into syrup by soaking it in water. It may also be purchased as a paste, which is easier to use. Although many recipes call for regular refined cane sugar, palm sugar is claimed to be more delicious. Coconut sugar and muscovado sugar have a similar taste and may be used as alternatives.

## Pandan Leaf

Bai toy hom, as it is known in Thai, adds perfume and taste to Thai meals. Pandan leaves are occasionally used to wrap meats and seafood. It may be used to flavor both savory and sweet meals, as well as beverages. If you can't locate the leaves, pandan extract will suffice.

## Sauce de plum

A sweet, sour, and spicy sauce that may be used as a dip or as a flavoring sauce for foods.

Rice

Sticky rice and jasmine rice are popular accompaniments to meat and veggie meals. It is also utilized in the preparation of snacks and sweets. Sticky rice is more popular in the north of Thailand, whereas jasmine rice is more popular in the south.

## Rhizome (Krachai or Gkrachai)

Ginger and galangal are both rhizomes, although lesser ginger, fingerroot, or Chinese ginger is thinner and smaller. It is not a well-known item in the West, yet it is used in salads, stir-fries, and Jungle Curry in traditional Thai cuisine. It has a moderately medicinal taste and is thought to be excellent for digestion. This may be available frozen or pickled in brine.

## Garlic with Shallots

These are frequently sautéed after being chopped or minced. They're utilized in a variety of meals.

Shrimp Paste (Kapi) is a staple in dips, sauces, and curry pastes. It is produced from powdered shrimp fermented in salt. It is used in the preparation of curry pastes and dipping sauces. It has a horrible odor, and some people incorrectly believe it is rotting or inedible.

**Sriracha Chili Sauce**

Chili, vinegar, garlic, and sugar are used to make this famous sauce. A Vietnamese immigrant created the Rooster brand, which is most popular in the United States. It is called after the Thai village of Si Racha, where the sauce originated.

**Sauce de Chili Sweet**

Nam chim kai is a common condiment in many Thai dishes, particularly appetizers. It's created using chiles, vinegar, and garlic.

Tamarind Mahahm is used to provide a sour flavor to meals. Although tamarind pods or pulp may be utilized, tamarind blocks or paste can also be purchased and are easier to use. Vinegar, lime juice, HP sauce, or dates smashed in lemon are all possible replacements.

**Thai basil**

A kind of sweet basil. Thai basil, also known as horapha, is reported to taste like a cross between anise and licorice. Although sweet basil may be replaced in recipes, this basil has a stronger heat tolerance than sweet basil. This is used in dishes such as Drunken Noodles (Pad Kee Mow) and curries. The most popular Thai herb is Holy Basil (kaphrao), which has a peppery, clove-like taste.

**Thai Chili Powder**

It's called prik Thai, and it's mostly made of white pepper, with a little coriander and garlic thrown in for good measure. Is utilized to provide an umami flavor.

**Vinegar**

Rice vinegar is often used to enhance the sourness of dishes or as an ingredient in dipping sauces and salad dressings. Although white distilled vinegar or apple cider vinegar may also be used, the taste will be somewhat different.

## Commonly Used Tools and Equipment

Thai cuisine does not need the use of specialist equipment. It is feasible to cook this cuisine with ingredients found in any regular kitchen. Here are several kitchen utensils that are typically seen in Thai households.

Wooden chopping blocks are used for cutting meat and fish.

## Cleaver

Typically, only one big knife is enough to make a range of cuts and slices for meats and vegetables. The flat side may be used to crush or smash garlic or ginger bits.

## Grater for coconut

This was formerly required for creating recipes needing coconut milk, but bottled coconut milk has rendered it obsolete. Those who want freshly produced coconut milk, on the other hand, may still find it in their kitchen. Freshly grated or frozen shredded coconut is also available.

## Spoon made from coconut shell

This is the traditional cooking ladle. However, any contemporary ladle will suffice.

Curry Pot A classic clay pot with big handles that is only used to make curry foods. Instead, a heavy-bottomed cooking pot may be utilized.

## Processor of Food

This will come in handy for making curry pastes and sauces. Using a mortar and pestle is more time-consuming and labor-intensive, but the finished taste is thought to be better.

## Basket of Glutinous Rice

A smart method of cooking and storing sticky rice. It is a bamboo basket that guarantees the rice has the proper stickiness and fluffiness. It also keeps the sticky rice from rotting, although it may be inconvenient for the contemporary chef. Instead, a splatter guard, fine-mesh metal sieve, or colander may be employed.

10

**Pestle and Mortar**

Traditionally fashioned of stone and used to smash garlic and bruise lemongrass leaves and plants. Also used in the preparation of curry pastes.

Grilling skewer made of bamboo.
Turner or spatula
This is very useful for stir-fries.

Steamer This is a common item in Thai kitchens and was historically used to boil sticky rice. The rice cooker is the current substitute.

**Strainer**

This strainer is useful for separating liquid or oil from other items such as noodles or fried meats.

**Wok**

The classic Asian cooking pan. It's great for stir-frying, deep-frying, and a variety of other culinary techniques. A wok may be replaced with any standard frying pan.


**Methods of Cooking**

Thai cuisine does not usually need the use of any sophisticated techniques. Thai recipes are often easy to make and require little oil.

**Stir-Frying**

A rapid, low-fat, and nutrient-dense cooking technique in which items are cooked in an ultra-hot wok with little oil and constant turning. As a consequence, you get a hot, fresh meal with crisp and flavorful components. The secret to successful stir-frying is, to begin with, a very hot wok before adding oil. Prepare all of the ingredients ahead of time and have them ready before you begin stir-frying. To seal in the juices, rapidly toss the fish.

11

## Steaming

The process of steaming locks in taste, nutrients, and freshness. To keep the steam in, place a heat-proof dish over boiling water and cover it with a tight-fitting lid.

## Stewing

Slow cooking is used in this approach to soften meats and lock in taste. The ingredients are chopped into equal sizes and covered with water before simmering. The liquid may be served as is or reduced to create the gravy.

## Frying in hot oil

This is normally done in a wok half-filled with oil. Before adding the frying ingredients, the oil must be heated to 350°F. Keep heat-resistant tongs, a slotted spoon, or a strainer on hand to fish the fried food from the hot oil. To keep the deep-fried food crisp, drain it on paper towels.

Grilling Meat and fish are sometimes grilled over coals or a flame. To give flavor and minimize charring, the dish is sometimes wrapped in pandan or banana leaves. Aluminum foil is now used by modern chefs. To guarantee consistent cooking, heat must be carefully controlled.

It's time to start cooking now that you've gathered your supplies and equipment.

# APPETIZERS

## Poh Pia Tod (Classic Spring Roll)

serves 8-16 people.
Time to prepare: 10 minutes + 20 minutes soaking time
Time to cook: 15-20 minutes

**Ingredients**
Sweet chili sauce
1 cup water, divided
4 teaspoons cornstarch
2 teaspoons fresh ginger, minced
1 teaspoon garlic, minced
4-6 pieces Thai chili, minced
1 cup rice vinegar
½ cup sugar
2 teaspoons ketchup

Sweet plum sauce
1 Japanese salted pickled plum
5 tablespoons sugar
1 tablespoon rice vinegar
2-3 tablespoons water

Spring rolls
4 dried shiitake mushrooms
3 ounces bean thread noodles

1 tablespoon vegetable oil
3 cloves garlic, minced
5 medium to large prawns, cleaned, peeled and minced (or about 3-
4 ounces ground pork or beef)
½ cup carrot, peeled and shredded
2 tablespoons soy sauce, preferably light
1 teaspoon sugar
½ teaspoon Thai pepper powder
1 cup fresh bean sprouts
2 tablespoons chopped spring onion
2 tablespoons chopped cilantro
16 fresh spring roll wrappers

Flour paste
2 tablespoons flour or cornstarch
1 tablespoon water


**Directions**
To make sweet chili sauce
1. Combine 1 tablespoon water and 1 tablespoon cornstarch in a cup or small dish. Set it aside for now.
2. In a mortar and pestle, pound the ginger, garlic, and chile to produce a paste. To prevent pepper burns, use rubber gloves while handling chili peppers.
3. Combine the vinegar, remaining water, sugar, and ketchup in a saucepan. Bring the water to a boil.
4. Reduce heat to low and cook for 5 minutes, stirring regularly.
5. Re-stir the water-cornstarch mixture, then whisk it into the sauce. Stir until the mixture thickens.
6. Turn off the heat.

To make sweet plum sauce
7. Mash all of the ingredients together in a small skillet or saucepan.
8. Bring them to a boil and keep them there until they form a syrup.

To make spring rolls

9. Soak the shiitake mushrooms for 10-20 minutes in boiling water.

Excess water should be drained and squeezed out. Set them aside after slicing them thinly.

10. Soak the noodles for 15 minutes in water. Drain and cut the strands into 1-inch lengths. Place aside.

11. Combine the flour paste ingredients in a small basin and keep them aside.

12. In a wok, heat the oil and sauté the garlic until aromatic.

13 Fold in the minced shrimp, shiitake mushrooms, noodles, and carrot.

14. Combine the soy sauce, sugar, and pepper powder in a mixing bowl. Cook for 3-5 minutes in a stir-fry pan.

15. Combine the bean sprouts, spring onion, and cilantro in a mixing bowl. Heat until well combined, then transfer to a bowl to cool.

16. Arrange one wrapper at a time in a diamond pattern on a clean surface or tray.

17. Place around 2 teaspoons of filler towards the bottom tip of the diamond or closest to you. If you put too much filling in the wrapper, it will break when cooking.

18. Fold the wrapper's bottom tip over the filling. Once, roll firmly.

19. Roll up to the top corner, folding the left and right corners inward.

20. To seal the roll, moisten the top corner with the flour paste.

21. Continue this method until all of the filling or wrappers have been used up.

22. Fry the spring rolls in approximately an inch of vegetable oil until golden brown. Fry in batches for more effective heating and crispier rolls, and do not overcrowd the rolls in the oil.

23. Remove the rolls from the oil using a spider strainer or tongs and lay them on a plate lined with paper towels.

24. Serve immediately with sweet-and-sour plum sauce or sweet chili sauce.

## Fried Sesame Tofu

4 servings
Time to prepare: 5-10 minutes + 20 minutes pressing time
Time to cook: 15–25 minutes

### Ingredients
12 ounces extra-firm tofu
1 egg, lightly beaten
¼ cup cornstarch
¼ cup peanut or vegetable oil
1-2 tablespoons sesame seeds, lightly toasted


For sauce
1 garlic clove, minced
½ cup sugar
2 tablespoons cornstarch
¾ cup water
⅛ cup rice vinegar
2 tablespoons soy sauce
16

2 tablespoons sesame oil
1 teaspoon chili paste

Peanut dipping sauce
½ cup cilantro, chopped
1 teaspoon chili pepper, ground to a paste
2 tablespoons peanuts, toasted and crushed
1 pinch salt
2 tablespoons sugar
2 tablespoons vinegar

**Directions**
1. Line a shallow baking pan with a tea towel and place the tofu in it.

Another towel is placed on top, followed by another baking pan. Add something heavy (such as a can of soup) to push down on for 20 minutes to extract the liquid. Drain and dry the tofu before cutting it into 2-inch squares that are half an inch thick and sliced in half.

2. Coat the cubes with cornstarch after dipping them in an egg. Shake to get rid of any extra cornstarch. Set aside the pieces by arranging them on a tray or dish.

3. In a small saucepan, combine the sauce ingredients.

Boil for 5 minutes, or until the sauce has thickened.

4. In the meanwhile, heat the oil in a wok. Fry the tofu for 3-5 minutes, or until the bottom is golden brown. Flip carefully to fry the other side. When the cubes are golden brown on all sides, take them to a plate lined with paper towels to drain.

5. Remove roughly a tablespoon of the oil from the pan. Pour the thickened sauce over the cooked tofu pieces in the pan.

Gently coat the tofu with the sauce and top with sesame seeds.

With dipping sauce, serve.

6. To create the dipping sauce, in a microwavable dish, mix the sugar, chili paste, salt, and vinegar and heat until the sugar is dissolved (about 1 minute). Stir thoroughly, then top with peanuts and cilantro.

17

# Tamarind Sauce on Fresh Summer Rolls

40-60 people (as snack or side dish)

Time to Prepare: 40 minutes
Time to cook: 2–5 minutes

## Ingredients
1 package of rice wrappers small, round

Filling
2 tablespoons soy sauce
1 tablespoon rice vinegar
1 tablespoon fish sauce
1 teaspoon brown, palm sugar, or muscovado
1 cup thin vermicelli rice noodles, cooked and rinsed in cold water,
drained
½ cup cooked shrimp, finely chopped
½ cup fried tofu, julienned
½ cup roasted chicken, shredded
1 cup lettuce, julienned
½ cup cucumber, julienned
½ cup fresh Thai basil, roughly chopped
½ cup fresh coriander, roughly chopped
¼ cup carrot, shredded or julienned
3-4 spring onions, finely chopped

Tamarind dipping sauce
½ cup water
18

½ teaspoon tamarind paste
2 teaspoons sugar
1 tablespoon soy sauce
1 tablespoon fish sauce
1 teaspoon arrowroot or cornstarch powder, dissolved in 3 tablespoons water
1 clove of garlic, minced
1 green or red chili, finely sliced


Directions

1. Make the dipping sauce first. In a saucepan, combine all of the ingredients. Bring to a near-boiling point and then turn off the heat.

Cook, continually stirring, until the sauce thickens.

As required, adjust the flavor. Take it off the fire and put it aside.

2. Place the rice wrapper aside.

3. Whisk together the soy sauce, vinegar, fish sauce, and sugar in a small basin. Set aside this mixture as well.

4. Combine all of the filling ingredients in a large mixing basin. Toss in the soy sauce mixture to coat.

5. Place a rice wrapper in hot water (it should be warm enough to touch). In 30 seconds, the wrapper should be soft enough.

6. Lay the wrapper on a clean, flat surface and immerse another wrapper from the box in boiling water.

7. Place a heaping spoonful of filling approximately half an inch from the wrapper's bottom. Form a tiny rectangular shape with the filling.

8. Fold the wrapper's bottom flap over the filling and tuck in the edges. As you roll from the bottom to the top, keep the roll tight. To seal, moisten the top flap with a little water.

9. Arrange the rolls on a dish, sealed side down. To expose the multicolored filling, cut the rolls diagonally in half.

10. Serve with tamarind sauce, if desired.

# Curry Puff serves 12-25 people.

Time to prepare: 20-30 minutes
Time to cook: 25-30 minutes

**Ingredients**
Cucumber relish
1 cup rice vinegar
6 tablespoons sugar
1-3 teaspoons chili paste
2 tablespoons cucumber, peeled and finely chopped
1 tablespoon fresh cilantro, finely chopped

For pastry dough
3 cups all-purpose flour, divided
6 tablespoons vegetable oil, plus more for frying
½ cup cold water

For filling
2 tablespoons vegetable oil
1 small onion, minced
1 teaspoon Thai pepper powder
1 tablespoon butter (optional)
1 ½ cups chicken fillet, cut into quarter- or half-inch cubes (For a
vegetable curry puff, omit the chicken, and add 1 cup each of cubed

carrots and green peas.)
1 ½ tablespoon curry powder
½ teaspoon cumin powder
2 teaspoons salt
1 tablespoon sugar
1 medium potato, peeled, cooked, and cut into cubes
1 teaspoon ground white pepper


**Directions**

1. Whisk together the vinegar, sugar, and chili paste for the cucumber relish. 2. Combine the cucumber and coriander in a mixing bowl. Refrigerate until ready to use, covered with plastic wrap.


In order to fill

2. Heat the oil in a wok over medium heat.

3. Combine the onion, Thai pepper powder, and butter in a mixing bowl (optional).

Sauté the onion until it is transparent.

4. Stir in the chicken. Cook, stirring occasionally until the chicken is nearly done, approximately 8-10 minutes.

5. Combine all of the spices, except the white pepper, in a large mixing bowl.

6. Add the potatoes and simmer until they absorb the majority of the liquid.

7. Taste and adjust as required. To avoid the dough from getting mushy or bursting, the filling should ideally be dry. It should be somewhat salty as well since the pastry will balance it out.

8. Remove from the heat and mix in the white pepper powder. Set it aside and let it cool.


To make pastry dough


21

9. Transfer 1 cup of the all-purpose flour to a separate bowl. You will have two bowls of flour, one with one cup and the other with two cups.

10. Pour a tablespoon of oil into each of the flour bowls. (As you go, be sure to add the same quantity of oil to each bowl.)

11. Using your hands, combine the oil and flour in the 1 cup flour basin. Continue mixing with your hand after adding another tablespoon of oil to each bowl. The contents of the second dish (containing 2 cups of flour) will be combined later.

12. Pour one-third of a spoonful of oil into each bowl. By now, the flour should be sticking together in the first bowl. This is referred to as "oil dough."

Set it aside for now.

13. Add the cold water to the second bowl and stir with one hand to produce a smooth, somewhat sticky dough. If necessary, add a bit more water. Divide the dough into 5 pieces that are nearly equal in size. Form them into balls, then flatten them with your palm and fingertips to make discs. This is referred to as "water dough."

14. Return to the first bowl of oil dough and divide it into 5 pieces as well. These are smaller than the preceding bowl's components.

15. Place one of the smaller pieces of oil dough in the middle of one of the water dough discs. Fold the disc's sides over the little dough ball and squeeze the borders together to seal.

Shape this dough "dumpling" into a ball, but do not knead it. Repeat with the remaining dough.

16. Roll out a ball of dough to approximately 14-inch thick using a rolling pin. Lift the bottom end of the dough and wrap it up like a scroll.

Place the "scroll" vertically on the table surface and flatten it with a rolling pin once more. Roll once more to create a scroll. This scroll should have a cylindrical form to it. Using a knife or dough cutter, cut this cylinder into 5 equal pieces. You will have 5 little discs and will be able to view the layers of water and oil dough that make up the disc.

17. Using a rolling pin, flatten out one of these discs into a thin circle approximately a sixteenth to an eighth-inch thick.

18. Place approximately 1 12 teaspoons to 1 tablespoon of filling (not too much or the pastry will break) towards the middle of the dough and fold it over to make a semi-circle with the filling inside. By gently rolling the edge with your thumb and fingers, you may flute or crimp the edges.

19. Heat the frying oil to 350°F (the dough will break apart if the oil is too hot) and deep-fry until golden brown.

20. Pat dry with paper towels. Toss with cucumber sauce and serve.

# Chicken Wings, Crispy

6 people
Time to prepare: 20 minutes, plus 6 hours marinating and 20 minutes air-drying.
Time to cook: 25 minutes

**Ingredients**
4 pounds of chicken wings
For the tamarind dipping sauce
½ cup water
½ teaspoon tamarind paste
2 teaspoons sugar
1 tablespoon soy sauce
1 tablespoon fish sauce
1 teaspoon arrowroot or cornstarch powder, dissolved in 3 tablespoons water
1 clove of garlic, minced
1 green or red chili, finely sliced

For marinade
6 large cloves of garlic, peeled
2 teaspoons whole coriander seeds
1 tablespoon whole white peppercorns
2 tablespoons cilantro roots or stems, finely chopped
3 tablespoons oyster sauce

24

2 teaspoons salt
1 teaspoon sugar

For batter
1 ½ cups rice flour
1 teaspoon salt
1 teaspoon chicken bouillon powder or granules
1 cup of water plus 2 teaspoons of baking soda

For dry coating
2 cups of rice flour

Directions

1. Make the dipping sauce first. In a saucepan, combine all of the ingredients. Bring it to a near-boiling point and then turn off the heat. Cook, stirring constantly until the sauce thickens.

As required, adjust the flavor. Take it off the fire and put it aside.

2. Place the chicken in a large mixing basin after drying it with paper towels.

3. Pound the first four marinade ingredients in a mortar and pestle or food processor to make a paste.

4. Toss the chicken with the paste and other marinade ingredients, and mix it in with your hands.

5. Cover and place in the refrigerator for 6 hours or overnight to marinate.

6. Combine the batter ingredients in a mixing bowl.

7. Coat the marinated chicken with the thin batter (do not drain or wipe off the marinade).

8. Immediately follow with a coat of rice flour. Shake off any excess flour before placing the breaded chicken on a pan or baking sheet.

9. Allow it to dry for 15-20 minutes.

10. In a wok or fryer, heat the oil to 350°F.

11. Fry the chicken until it is well cooked on the inside and golden brown on the exterior.

12. Remove from the oil and place on a cooling rack lined with paper towels to drain.

13. Toss with tamarind dipping sauce and serve.

# Cake of Thai Fish

Serves: 10 to 15
Time to prepare: 20 minutes
Time to cook: 10 minutes


**Ingredients**
Cucumber Relish
¾ cup Thai sweet chili sauce
½ cup cucumber, thinly sliced
2 tablespoons dry-roasted peanuts, finely chopped
2 tablespoon cilantro leaves, coarsely chopped
3 tablespoon shallots, thinly sliced

2 large egg whites
1 (4-ounce) can of red curry paste
¼ cup sugar

4 tablespoons fish sauce
1 tablespoon paprika (optional)
1 ½ pounds fish paste (store-bought)
4 tablespoons chiffonade of kaffir lime leaves
1 cup Chinese long beans, finely chopped
½ cup chiffonade of basil leaves
Vegetable oil, for deep-frying

**Directions**

1. Make the cucumber relish first. Refrigerate the relish after combining all of the ingredients.

2. In the meanwhile, combine the egg whites, red curry paste, sugar, fish sauce, and paprika, if used. Mix in the fish paste until it forms a thick paste. Mix with your hands or the paddle attachment of a stand mixer. For around 5 minutes, combine all of the ingredients in a mixing bowl.

3. When the paste is fully combined and sticky, fold in the kaffir lime leaves, long beans, and basil chiffonade.

4. Wrap in plastic wrap and place in the refrigerator for 30 minutes.

5. Heat a wok over medium heat and fill it approximately 2 inches deep with oil. The oil's temperature should be 350°F.

6. Prepare a small dish of water in which to moisten your hands so that the fish paste does not adhere to them.

7. Scoop out a handful of the fish paste mixture after soaking your hands. Form a ball and flatten it into a 2-inch-diameter patty.

8. Fry the fish patties in hot oil until golden brown (about 30 seconds). Cook the other side by flipping the pan over. After approximately 1 minute of cooking, the patties should be done. When the patties resist or bounce when tapped during frying, they are done.

9. Remove the cooked fish cakes and pat them dry with paper towels.

10. Garnish with cucumber relish and serve. It may also be served with rice.

# Calamari Crispy Fried b

4-6 people
Time to Prepare: 10 minutes
Time to cook: 10 minutes.


**Ingredients**
1 pound squid tubes, cut into ½-inch rings (or use pre-cut rings)

2 cups semolina flour, divided
1 tablespoon teaspoon salt
1 tablespoon sugar
1-2 teaspoons dried crushed chilies or cayenne powder
1 teaspoon garlic powder
⅛ teaspoon 5-spice powder (optional)
⅛ teaspoon ground white pepper (optional)
2 eggs, lightly beaten
Vegetable oil for frying
Lettuce or fresh coriander leaves for serving
Lime wedges, for serving (optional)


Directions

1. Using a towel, dry the squid rings.

2. Make three bowls. 1 cup of flour should be placed in the first bowl. The beaten eggs should be placed in the second bowl. Combine the remaining flour, salt, sugar, and spices in the third bowl. This is the coating solution.

3. Make a tray for the coated rings.

4. Coat a ring in plain flour, shaking lightly to remove any excess.

5. Next, dip it into the egg, followed by the coating mixture.

Place it on the tray. If the coated rings come into contact with each other, they will cling together.

7. Continue until all of the rings are covered.

8. pour 1 inch of oil into a wok or frying pan. Preheat the oven to 350°F on medium-high. When the oil starts to shimmer, test it by inserting a ring into the oil; it should sizzle and fry.

9. Fry the rings in batches for approximately 12 minutes on each side, to minimize overcrowding and to maintain the proper frying temperature. To turn the rings, use a skewer.

10. If the oil becomes too hot, it may spatter, so adjust the heat as needed.

11. The fried rings should have a light golden brown color. If you overcook the squid, it will become rubbery.

12. Pat the cooked rings dry with paper towels.

13. Drizzle with Thai sweet chili sauce and serve immediately.

# Cake with Andaman Shrimp

Serve: 4-6 people
Time to Prepare: 10 minutes
Time to cook: 20 minutes.

## Ingredients
7 ounces pork belly, cubed
5-6 cloves garlic, minced
1 teaspoon ground white pepper
1 cilantro root
1 pound of shrimp meat
2 eggs
4 teaspoons sugar
2 tablespoons light soy sauce
⅓ cup all-purpose flour
2 cups Panko bread crumbs
Oil for frying

## Directions

1. In a food processor, combine the pork belly, garlic, pepper, and cilantro root and crush to a coarse consistency.

2. Place 1/3 of the shrimp, eggs, sugar, soy sauce, and flour in a food processor and pulse until the mixture is gritty but uniformly distributed.

3. Add the remaining shrimp and pulse the food processor a few times to combine.

4. To test, microwave a tablespoon for 15 seconds. Make any necessary modifications to the saltiness, sweetness, or spiciness. If it's too dry, add more water.

5. Using your hands, form 2 teaspoons of the shrimp mixture into a patty and cover with Panko bread crumbs.

6. Fry in a 1-inch deep oil at 300°F, rotating occasionally.

7. You must control the temperature so that the patty cooks evenly. The cake is done when it is golden brown on the exterior and thoroughly done on the interior.

8. Pat dry with paper towels.

9. Toss with sweet plum sauce or sweet chili sauce and serve.

## Rangoon with Crab

Serve: 8-10 people
Time to Prepare: 10 minutes
Time to cook: 2 minutes

**Ingredients**
1 (6-ounce) can of crabmeat

6 ounces cream cheese, softened to room temperature
3 cloves garlic, minced
1 dash Worcestershire sauce
½ teaspoon salt
1 dash of white pepper
Wonton skins
1 beaten egg, for sealing
Oil, for frying

## Directions

1. In a mixing bowl, combine the first 6 ingredients (through white pepper), stirring thoroughly.

2. Prepare the wontons and layout a clean wrapper.

3. For each wonton, measure out around 12 teaspoons of filling. Place a wonton in the center and press the opposing edges together.

4. Carefully press out any air (this is critical because the filling would explode while frying) and then seal the borders with the beaten eggs.

5. Fry until golden brown in a deep fryer, then drain on paper towels.

6. Garnish with sweet chili sauce or peanut sauce if desired.

# Chicken Satay

servings : 3-4  people
Time to prepare: 30 minutes + 4 hours marinating
Time to cook: 8-10 minutes

## Ingredients

Peanut-coconut milk sauce
1 tablespoon dark soy sauce
1 small onion, minced
½ cup peanut butter
2 tablespoons brown sugar
1 cup coconut milk
1 teaspoon Sriracha or red pepper flakes, or to taste
Salt, as needed
2 tablespoons peanuts, toasted and crushed
2 teaspoons honey, or to taste (optional)

For satay
2 pounds of chicken breast fillets (you may also use pork or beef)
1 tablespoon ground coriander
1 tablespoon curry powder
2 teaspoons cumin powder
½ teaspoon turmeric powder
½ teaspoon pepper
¼ cup sugar

33

2 teaspoons salt
6 cloves garlic, peeled
¼ cup lemongrass, roughly chopped
¼ cup cilantro, roughly chopped
½ cup coconut milk
3-4 tablespoons condensed milk
1 tablespoon vegetable oil


Instructions for making peanut-coconut milk sauce

1. Whisk together all of the ingredients EXCEPT the crushed peanuts and honey in a saucepan (optional).

2. Bring to a boil over medium-high heat, stirring or whisking constantly.

3. Take the pan from the heat.

4. Adjust the flavor with extra chili sauce or salt to taste. If desired, drizzle with honey.

5. Stir in the peanuts. It may be used either heated or at room temperature.


To make satay

6. Trim the chicken, removing any excess fat or cartilage.

7. Slice the meat into 2-inch by 1-inch pieces.

8. Butterfly the strips by cutting a 14-inch thick strip horizontally up to around 14-inch from the joint of the meat. Cut the thicker section from the 'joint' outward to lengthen again. As a result, you will get a long piece of chicken flesh that is roughly 5-6 inches long and 14 inches thick. Repeat with the remaining chicken.

9. Combine the meat with the coriander, curry, cumin, turmeric, and pepper powders in a mixing dish. Mix in the sugar and salt. Set aside after thoroughly mixing.

10. Combine the garlic, lemongrass, cilantro, and coconut milk in a blender. Blend until completely smooth.

11. Drizzle the coconut milk mixture over the chicken.

12 Stir in the condensed milk and oil.

13. Using your hands, combine everything until fully combined.

14 Cover with plastic wrap, place in the refrigerator and let marinate for 4 hours overnight.

15. Using a kitchen knife, trim the skewered chicken's edges so they don't dangle.

16. When grilling, use any remaining marinade as a glaze.

17. Grill the skewers for 4-5 minutes on each side over medium-low heat, brushing with marinade as needed. When the satay is done, it will seem dry.

18. If preferred, serve with peanut-coconut milk sauce or peanut dipping sauce and toasted bread.

# SOUPS

## Soup with Spicy Lemongrass (Tom Yum)

servings : 3-4  people
Time to Prepare: 5 minutes
Time to cook: 30 minutes


**Ingredients**
1 teaspoon soy sauce
1 teaspoon white sugar
1 teaspoon red curry paste, or to taste
4 cups water
2 stalks of lemon grass, sliced
4-6 kaffir lime leaves
1 bunch Bok choy, leaves separated, each leaf halved
½ cup baby corn, sliced
¼ cup carrot, diced small
1 medium tomato, sliced
3-4 ounces mushrooms, roughly chopped
1 red bell pepper, diced small
2 tablespoons lime juice
Salt to taste
1 tablespoon Thai basil leaves, for garnish

**Directions**

1. In a cup or dish, combine the soy sauce, sugar, and red curry paste. Set it aside for now.

2. In a saucepan, heat the water and add the lemongrass. Drop the lime leaves into the water after tearing them.

3. Bring to a boil for 5 minutes, or until the water becomes green and aromatic.

4. Remove the lemongrass and lime leaves from the stock and return them to the pot.

5. Combine the Bok choy, baby corn, carrot, tomato, mushrooms, and bell pepper in a mixing bowl.

6. Bring the water to a boil. Cook, stirring occasionally until the veggies are soft but not overdone.

7. Stir in the soy sauce-lime juice combination.

8. Season with salt and adjust the flavor to your liking. Tom Yum should have a sour and spicy flavor. As required, add extra lime juice or red curry paste.

9. Garnish with Thai basil and serve hot.

Coconut Soup in Minutes (Tom Kha)

Serves: 2 people
Time to Prepare: 10 minutes
Time to cook: 10 minutes

**Ingredients**
1 (14-ounce) can of coconut milk
2 cups chicken stock
1 1-inch piece of ginger, peeled and chopped
1 pound shrimp, cleaned, shelled, and deveined OR chicken breast,
trimmed and sliced OR a combination of both
1 cup mushrooms, cleaned and sliced
2 tablespoons fresh lime juice
Zest of 1 lemon or lime
1 tablespoon fish sauce
1 teaspoon chili paste or Sriracha
For garnish
Green onion, chopped
Cilantro, chopped

**Directions**

1. In a saucepan, bring the coconut milk, chicken stock, and ginger to a boil, then lower to a simmer.

2. Add the other ingredients (excluding the garnishes) and bring to a boil.

Cook for 5 minutes if using shrimp, or 10 minutes if using chicken. If using both, sauté the chicken for 5 minutes before adding the shrimp and simmering for another 5 minutes.

3. Taste and add extra fish sauce, chili, or Sriracha if desired.

4. Garnish with green onion and cilantro and serve hot.

# SALAD

## Salad with papaya (Som Tum)

Servings: 2 PEOPLE
Preparation Time: 20 minutes
Cooking Time: 5 minutes, or none at all

**Ingredients**
2 cups shredded green papaya
2 cloves garlic, peeled
1 tablespoon dried shrimp (optional)
1-3 fresh birds eye chilies
½ piece palm sugar OR 1 tablespoon sugar
½ cup chopped tomato, preferably cherry
1-2 tablespoons green beans, topped and sliced thinly, 1 inch in

length
Juice of 1 lime or lemon
1 ½ tablespoons fish sauce

2 tablespoons toasted peanuts, crushed

Directions

1. To produce a thick syrup using palm sugar, melt it in a skillet with 2 tablespoons of water over low heat. Remove it from the oven and set it aside to cool.

2. Crush the garlic and dried shrimp in a mortar and pestle (optional). After that, add the chili. Crush but do not purée the fruit. If your mortar and pestle are big enough, add the green papaya and pound it to integrate the taste. If not, just combine the papaya, smashed garlic, shrimp, and chile in a mixing bowl.

3. Combine the liquid palm sugar (or sugar), tomatoes, beans, lime juice, and fish sauce in a mixing bowl. To integrate flavors, properly combine all ingredients.

4. Garnish with crushed peanuts before serving.

## Salad with Thai BBQ Beef

4 servings
Preparation Time required: 20 minutes + 4 hours marinating
Time to cook: 10 minutes

**Ingredients**
1 pound beef steak, sliced about 1 to 1 ½-inches thick
For marinade or dressing (to be divided)
3 tablespoons lime juice, divided
3 tablespoons soy sauce
3 tablespoons vegetable oil
2 tablespoons brown sugar
3 cloves garlic, minced
1 ½ teaspoons ginger, minced
1 ¼ teaspoons red curry paste or chili-garlic sauce

For salad
½ head red-leaf lettuce, torn
½ red bell pepper, trimmed and julienned
½ cucumber, seeded and julienned
½ cup cilantro leaves rinsed and dried
1 cup chiffonade of basil leaves
3 shallots, thinly sliced, divided, for garnish

**Directions**
1. Using paper towels, pat the meat dry.

2. In a mixing dish, combine the marinade/dressing ingredients. To blend the flavors, thoroughly combine all of the ingredients in a mixing bowl. Divide the mixture in half and set aside half for dressing. Refrigerate.

3. Add the remaining half to the meat and refrigerate for 4 hours overnight.

4. Grill the marinated meat until medium-rare (approximately 5 minutes on each side) or until done to preference. Remove from the heat and set aside to cool.

5. Thinly slice the meat against the grain.

6. Combine the remaining ingredients, reserving some shallots for decoration.

7. Toss the ingredients in the dressing to coat.

8. Garnish with the reserved shallots and serve.

41

# Salad of Thai Tofu and Chicken with Peanut Dressing

2 people
Time to Prepare: 5 minutes
Time to cook: 5-10 minutes


**Ingredients**
Peanut dressing
3 tablespoons water
2 tablespoons rice wine vinegar
1 tablespoon green onions, chopped
1 tablespoon peanut butter
1 tablespoon soy sauce
1 teaspoon ginger, peeled and grated
1 teaspoon Sriracha or chili sauce
1 teaspoon dark sesame oil
2 teaspoons dry-roasted peanuts


For salad
3 ounces extra-firm tofu
2 cups mixed baby salad greens
½ cup fresh bean sprouts
2 tablespoons red onion, vertically sliced
2 tablespoons fresh mint leaves
2 tablespoons fresh cilantro leaves
1 medium carrot, peeled and julienned
4 cherry tomatoes, quartered

1 cup cooked chicken breast, shredded

**Directions**

1. To make the dressing, first set aside the peanuts and then combine the other ingredients in a blender. Blend until completely smooth. Blend for roughly 10 seconds, just to smash the peanuts. Alternatively, grind the peanuts in a mortar and pestle ahead of time and sprinkle them over the dressing. Place aside.

2. Fry the tofu on both sides until golden brown. Drain the pasta and chop it into bite-size pieces. Set it aside for now. To obtain a crisper texture, you might cut the tofu prior to frying it.

3. To make the salad, combine all of the ingredients. Toss in the dressing to coat evenly.

4. Top with fried tofu pieces and serve.

# RICE AND NOODLES

## Pad Thai with chicken

serves: 4 people
Time to Prepare: 10 minutes
Time to cook: 15 minutes

### Ingredients
1 (8-ounce) box pad Thai rice noodles
10 tablespoons pad Thai sauce, store-bought OR make your

own

3 tablespoons vegetable oil, divided
3 cloves garlic, minced
1 shallot, finely sliced
8 ounces chicken breast fillet, trimmed and sliced thinly
2 eggs
1 cup bean sprouts
Pad Thai sauce ingredients
3 tablespoons soy sauce
1 tablespoon chili sauce or Sriracha
1 tablespoon tamarind paste OR 2 tablespoons lime juice
1 tablespoon fish sauce

2 tablespoons palm sugar or brown sugar
2 tablespoons vegetable or peanut oil
For garnish
Cilantro, chopped
Lime wedges
Toasted peanuts, crushed

## Directions

1. Soak the noodles for approximately 10 minutes in hot (not boiling) water before draining (or following the instructions on the package). Place aside.

2. If you're not using store-bought pad Thai sauce, combine the sauce ingredients in a dish and leave them aside.

3. Melt the butter in a wok over high heat. Sauté the garlic, shallots, and chicken in 2 tablespoons of oil.

4. Cook for approximately 10 minutes, or until the chicken is done. Take out of the wok.

5. Scramble the eggs in the remaining oil in the wok.

6. Reduce the heat to low and add the pad Thai sauce, followed by the noodles, tossing to coat evenly.

7. Stir in the chicken mixture until well cooked.

8. Garnish with cilantro, peanuts, and lime wedges.

# See Ew Chicken Pad

Serves : 3 people
Time to Prepare: 10 minutes
Time to cook: 5 minutes


**Ingredients**
1 (8-ounce) pack of rice stick noodles or Sen Yai Noodles
For sauce
2 tablespoons dark soy sauce (or 1 ½ tablespoons soy sauce +

tablespoon honey)
2 tablespoons oyster sauce
2 teaspoons soy sauce
2 teaspoons white vinegar
2 teaspoons sugar
2 tablespoons water
Stir-fry
2 tablespoons peanut or vegetable oil
2 cloves garlic, smashed
1 cup skinless chicken thighs or breast fillet, cut into bite-sized
pieces
Broccoli stems, julienned

1 large egg

4 cups Chinese broccoli (or you can use Bok choy or pak Choy),

separate leaves from stems

**Directions**

1. Soak the noodles for approximately 10 minutes in hot (not boiling) water before draining (or following the packaging instructions). Place aside.

2. Whisk together the sauce ingredients and leave them aside.

3. Heat the oil in a wok over high heat and add the crushed garlic.

As the pan heated up, crush the garlic to mince it.

4. Add the chicken and broccoli stems when the oil is heated and the garlic is golden brown. 1 minute of stirring

5. Push the garlic, broccoli, and chicken to the side of the pan while scrambling the egg in the oil. There will be some charring, which will add taste.

6. Stir in the noodles, broccoli leaves, and sauce.

7. Toss to evenly coat, and cook until the leaves begin to wilt.

8. Take the pan from the heat and serve.

**Drunken Noodles (Pad Kee Mao)**

serves: 2-3 people
Time to Prepare: 10 minutes
Time to cook: 5 minutes

**Ingredients**
1 (7-ounce) pack pad Thai noodles, dried

For sauce
3 tablespoons oyster sauce
3 tablespoons regular soy sauce (or 1:1 dark to light soy sauce)
2 teaspoons sugar
2 tablespoons water

For stir-fry
2 tablespoons peanut or vegetable oil
3 large cloves garlic, minced
1-3 birds' eye chilies, deseeded and very finely chopped
10 ounces chicken thigh or breast fillet, cut into bite-sized pieces
1 cup basil leaves, preferably holy basil (kaphrao)
2 shallot stems, cut into 2-inch pieces
½ cup carrot, julienned
½ cup canned bamboo shoots, rinsed and drained (if using precooked, vacuum packed, open pack just before use, rinse and cut)
¼ red bell pepper, deseeded and julienned

**Directions**
1. Soak the noodles for approximately 10 minutes in hot (not boiling) water before draining (or following the packaging instructions). Place aside.

2. In a small dish, whisk together the sauce ingredients and put aside.

3. Heat the oil in a wok or frying pan over high heat. Cook for 10 seconds after adding the garlic and chiles.

4. Add the chicken and stir-fry for 2-3 minutes, or until done.

48

5. Stir in the shallot stalks, carrot, and approximately 1 tablespoon of sauce to coat the chicken.

6. Cook until the noodles, bamboo shoots, bell pepper, and remaining sauce are equally covered. If the noodles are too dry, mix in a tablespoon (or more, if necessary) of hot water.

7. Remove from the heat. Stir in the basil leaves to wilt them in the heated noodles.

8. Plate and serve.

## Glass Noodles Stir-Fried (Pad Woon Sen)

serves: 4peole
Time to prepare: 20 minutes
Time to cook: 15 minutes

## Ingredients
6 ounces glass of bean noodles (woon sen)
For the sauce
3 tablespoons fish sauce
3 tablespoons Sriracha sauce
1 tablespoon oyster sauce
1 tablespoon rice wine vinegar
½ teaspoon sesame oil

49

For the noodles
3 tablespoons peanut oil, divided
2 eggs
Pinch of salt
1 small yellow onion, julienned
2 stalks of celery, sliced thin on the bias
3 garlic cloves, crushed and minced
1 small carrot, peeled and julienned
2 shallot stems, cut into 2-inch pieces
1 cup Napa cabbage, finely sliced
2 chicken fillets, trimmed and cut into very thin strips

**Directions**

1. Soak the noodles for approximately 10 minutes in hot (but not boiling) water (or follow the packaging instructions). Set aside after draining.

2. Beat the eggs well with a dash of salt.

3. Whisk together the sauce ingredients in a small dish and leave aside.

4. Melt the butter in a wok over medium heat. Swirl in 2 tablespoons of peanut oil to coat the pan.

5. Stir in the beaten eggs and simmer for approximately 1 minute.

Place the cooked eggs on a cutting board and cut them into ribbons. Place aside.

6. Add roughly a teaspoon more oil to the same pan and heat nearly to the smoking point.

7. Cook the onion until it is transparent. Stir-fry the celery for 30 seconds.

8. Stir in the garlic for 15 seconds.

9. If necessary, add another teaspoon of oil to the pan. Stir in the carrots and shallots for approximately 1 minute.

10. Cook until the Napa cabbage starts to wilt. Remove the vegetable combination from the pan and place it on a plate.

11. Add any residual oil to the same wok as required. Allow it to cook for approximately 15 seconds before adding the chicken pieces. Stir-fry until the chicken is cooked through.

12. Stir in the drained noodles and roughly two-thirds of the sauce. Toss and cook until the noodles are well covered and the liquid has been absorbed. If necessary, adjust the saltiness.

13. Spoon the noodle-chicken combination into a serving dish. Combine the remaining sauce, veggies, and egg ribbons in a mixing bowl. To coat evenly, toss everything together.

14th, serve

## Thai Fried Rice

serves 4-6 people.
Time to Prepare: 5 minutes
Time to cook: 15-20 minutes

**Ingredients**
4 cups pre-cooked cold jasmine rice
3-4 tablespoons peanut oil or vegetable oil

51

4 cloves garlic, minced
1 ½ cups boneless skinless chicken breast fillets (lean pork or beef
maybe used), thinly sliced
2 eggs, beaten and seasoned with salt and pepper
¾ cup snow peas, trimmed
½ cup carrot, julienned
4 green onions, sliced thin
1 tomato, chopped
2 teaspoons palm sugar or table sugar
3 tablespoons Thai fish sauce
1 tablespoon oyster sauce
1-3 teaspoons chili sauce, or according to taste
For garnish
½ cup cilantro, chopped
1 cucumber, sliced
2 limes, cut into wedges

**Directions**

1. Separate the grains of chilled rice with a wooden spoon or your hands (this is preferable). Use plastic gloves or moisten your hands to keep the rice from sticking. Set it aside for now.

2. Melt the butter in a large wok or nonstick pan over medium-high heat.

3. Swirl in the oil, then add the garlic and stir-fry for 30 seconds.

4. Stir-fry the chicken pieces until they are cooked through.

5. Transfer to the side of the wok and add extra oil if necessary. Allow the oil to reheat for around 15 seconds.

6. Add the beaten egg and scramble it.

7. Stir in the snow peas and carrots for around 45 seconds.

8. Add the rice, scooping from the bottom up to ensure equal cooking. You should be able to smell the rice toasting.

9. Combine the spring onions, tomato, sugar, and sauces in a mixing bowl. Continue to stir-fry the rice to coat it with flavor.

10. Garnish with cilantro, cucumbers, and lime wedges, and serve with fish and chili sauces on the side.

## Fried Pineapple Rice

Serves : 5 people
Time to Prepare: 30 minutes
Time to cook: 10 minutes

**Ingredients**
4 cups cold, precooked rice
2-3 tablespoons peanut or vegetable oil, divided
2 shallots, finely chopped
3 cloves garlic, finely chopped
1 red or green chili, thinly sliced
2-4 tablespoons vegetable or chicken stock
2 eggs, beaten and seasoned with salt and pepper
½ cup frozen peas (optional)
1 small carrot, julienned (optional)
1 ½ cups pineapple chunks, canned or fresh, drained
¼ cup raisins

53

½ cup roasted, unsalted whole cashew nuts
For sauce
1 tablespoon fish sauce
2 tablespoons soy sauce
2 teaspoons curry powder
½ teaspoon sugar
For garnish
3 stalks spring onion, chopped
⅓ cup fresh cilantro, chopped

**Directions**
1. Separate the grains of chilled rice with a wooden spoon or your hands (this is preferable). Use plastic gloves or moisten your hands to keep the rice from sticking. Set it aside for now.

2. In a small dish or cup, combine the sauce ingredients. Set things aside for now.

3. In a large wok or nonstick skillet, heat the oil over medium-high heat.

4. Pour in 2 teaspoons of oil.

5. Cook for 1 minute, or until the shallots, garlic, and chile are aromatic. To deglaze, add 1 tablespoon of stock to sizzle.

Place it on the edge of the wok.

6. Scramble the beaten eggs in the middle of the wok.

7. Add the peas and carrots (if using) at this stage. If necessary, add stock a tablespoon at a time to keep the mixture from drying out. 1 minute of stirring

8. If necessary, add another tablespoon of oil and let to heat.

9. Combine the rice, pineapple chunks, raisins, and cashew nuts in a mixing bowl.

10. Stir in the prepared sauce over medium-high to high heat to mix. Constantly "scoop" the rice with a spatula from the bottom up. After around 5 minutes, the rice should produce soft popping noises.

11. Taste and season with salt or chili sauce to taste. If desired, a few drops of lime juice may be added to lessen the saltiness.

12. Traditionally, this meal is served in a carved-out pineapple.
Garnish with cilantro and spring onions if desired.
55

# MAIN COURSES OF CHICKEN AND DUCK

## Chicken Coconut Green Curry Made Simple

serves:  8  people
Preparation Time: 5 minutes (does not include making the curry paste)
Time to cook: 15 minutes

**Ingredients** :
Green Curry Paste
4-6 green chilies, seeded and chopped
2 shallots, chopped
1 tablespoon ginger, peeled and grated
2 cloves garlic, crushed
1 bunch cilantro
2 stalks of lemongrass, bruised

Zest of 1 lime
Juice of 1 lime
8 kaffir lime leaves, torn
1 tablespoon galangal, peeled and chopped
1 tablespoon coriander seeds, crushed
1 teaspoon ground cumin
1 teaspoon black peppercorns, crushed
2 teaspoon fish sauce
4 tablespoons peanut or vegetable oil

For curry
2 tablespoons vegetable oil
2-3 tablespoons green curry paste (homemade or store-bought)
1 ½ pound boneless chicken thigh or breast fillet, cut into 1-inch
pieces
3 cups coconut cream or coconut milk (about 2 cans)
1 cup string beans, topped and cut into 1 ½- to 2-inch pieces
½ medium carrot, peeled and thinly sliced
4 ounces bamboo shoot, canned or vacuum-packed, drained and
sliced
1 medium Japanese eggplant, cut into 2-inch pieces
½ cup mixed bell peppers (red and green), seeded and cut into
bite-size pieces
1 tablespoon fish sauce, or to taste
1 teaspoon sugar, or to taste
Soy sauce, to taste (optional)

Green curry paste preparation instructions

To prevent pepper burns, use rubber gloves while handling chili peppers.

1. Pound or pound the lemongrass in a mortar and pestle before combining it with the other ingredients in a food processor.

Keep it refrigerated in a glass container.

To make curry

2. In a big wok, saucepan, or Dutch oven, heat the oil over medium heat.

3. Cook the curry paste until it is aromatic (about 2 minutes). Avoid inhaling the fumes or smoke, since they might induce coughing.

4. Add the chicken pieces and simmer for approximately 5 minutes, enabling the curry flavor to penetrate the meat.

5. Add the coconut cream or milk and simmer for 10-15 minutes, or until the chicken is done and the oil separates from the coconut cream on the top.

6. Add the veggies and simmer for another 5 minutes, or until the vegetables are soft and the sauce has thickened.

7. Season with fish sauce, sugar, and soy sauce to taste (optional). If you want additional curry taste, sauté extra curry paste in a tiny quantity of oil before adding it to the stew.

Serve with rice.

## Chicken in Red Curry

Serves: 2
Preparation Time: 5 minutes (does not include the preparation of the curry paste)
Time to cook: 15 minutes

**Ingredients**
Red Curry Paste
15-20 dried hot red chilies (prik haeng), seeded and chopped
4 teaspoons coriander seeds
2 stalks of fresh lemongrass, outer leaves removed
1 teaspoon black peppercorns
4 teaspoons galangal, peeled and chopped
6 kaffir lime leaves, finely chopped
2 tablespoons cilantro roots or stems, chopped
5 small shallots, chopped
¼ cup garlic, chopped
15-20 fresh red birds-eye chilies (prik kii noo), finely chopped
2 teaspoons Thai shrimp paste (Kapi)
½ teaspoon salt

For curry
1 ½ tablespoons peanut or vegetable oil
2-3 tablespoons red curry paste (homemade or store-bought), or to
taste
8 ounces chicken breast, cut into bite-sized pieces (you may also
use beef, pork or shrimp)
½ cup coconut milk
½ cup chicken stock or water
½ medium carrot, peeled and sliced thinly
4 ounces bamboo shoot, canned or vacuum-packed, drained and
sliced
1 medium Japanese eggplant, cut into 2-inch pieces
5 kaffir lime leaves, lightly bruised
2 pieces red chili, cut into thick strips
1 tablespoon fish sauce
1 teaspoon sugar or palm sugar, or to taste
¼ cup Thai basil leaves
½ small green bell pepper, seeded and cut into bite-size pieces
(optional)
½ small red bell pepper, seeded and cut into bite-size pieces
(optional)

Instructions for making red curry paste

To prevent pepper burns, use rubber gloves while handling chili peppers.

1. Soak the dried, chopped chilies for approximately 20 minutes in water.

Drain thoroughly.

2. Heat a pan over medium heat and roast the coriander for 3 minutes, or until aromatic.

3. Pound the coriander and peppercorns in a mortar and pestle, then put aside.

4. Thinly slice the lemongrass stalks and pound them in a mortar and pestle.

5. In a mixing bowl, combine the lemongrass, galangal, lime leaves, cilantro, shallots, garlic, fresh chilies, and soaking dried chilies.

Combine the shrimp paste and salt in a mixing bowl. Blend the contents in three batches in a food processor, adding 12 tablespoons of water each batch, until it forms a smooth paste.

6. Pulse in the shrimp paste and salt to combine.

7. Place it in little glass jars to keep it fresh. Store in the refrigerator.

To make curry

8. Heat the oil in a wok or saucepan over medium heat.

9. Heat the red curry paste until it is aromatic.

10. Stir in the chicken, making sure all of the curry flavor is absorbed.

11. Add the coconut milk and water or stock, and bring to a boil for 2 minutes.

12 Stir in the carrots, beans, bamboo shoots, eggplant, kaffir lime leaves, and red chile.

13. Turn down the heat. Cover the saucepan and cook for 10 minutes, or until the sauce thickens.

14. Combine the fish sauce, sugar, basil leaves, and bell peppers in a mixing bowl (optional). Stir.

15. Season with fish sauce, sugar, and soy sauce to taste (optional). If you want a stronger curry paste, sauté extra curry paste in a tiny quantity of oil before adding it to the stew.

Serve with rice.

## Chicken in Panang Curry

4 servings
Preparation Time: 15 minutes, plus 30 minutes to make homemade Panang curry paste.
Time to cook: 20 minutes.

**Ingredients**
Panang Curry Paste
2 tablespoons lemongrass, sliced thin
1 tablespoon coriander seeds, toasted
½ teaspoon cumin seeds, toasted
2 tablespoons black peppercorns, crushed
1 tablespoon galangal, peeled and chopped
6 kaffir lime leaves, chopped
2 tablespoons cilantro root, peeled and chopped
1 teaspoon salt

61

2 shallots, sliced thin
5 cloves garlic, chopped
1 teaspoon shrimp paste
4 pieces of mace, toasted
2 cardamom pods, toasted
4 large green peppers, roasted
10 big red dried chilies, soaked in water for 10 minutes.

**Panang curry paste preparation instructions**

1. In a mortar and pestle, pound the first four ingredients one at a time.

2. In a food processor, combine all of the ingredients and mix until smooth. You may also pound everything with a big mortar and pestle, adding ingredients one at a time, but the taste is better than when using a food processor.

To prevent pepper burns, use rubber gloves while handling chili peppers.

3. Refrigerate and store in glass jars.

To make curry

4. Heat the oil in a wok or saucepan over medium heat.

5. Cook till the Panang curry paste is aromatic.

6. Add the coconut milk and bring to a boil for approximately 2 minutes.

7. Add the chicken and cook, turning often, until the chicken is done, approximately 10-15 minutes.

8. Combine the string beans, carrot, sugar, fish sauce, kaffir lime leaves, and bell pepper in a mixing bowl.

9. Turn down the heat. Cover the saucepan and let it boil for 5 minutes, or until the sauce thickens.

10. Taste and adjust the flavor with extra fish sauce if required.

11. Remove from the heat and top with the chile and Thai basil.

12. Serve with white rice.

# Jungle Curry

4 servings
Time to Prepare: 8 minutes
Time to cook: 20 minutes


## Ingredients
1 cup water or chicken stock
1-3 tablespoons red curry paste (homemade or store-bought), or
according to taste
1 1-inch piece of fresh galangal, peeled and sliced or grated
1 teaspoon rhizome (optional), skin scraped off and thinly sliced
1 pound chicken thighs or breast fillet, thinly sliced
2 tablespoons fish sauce
1 teaspoon sugar
½ medium carrot, peeled and thinly sliced
½ cup bamboo shoots (canned or vacuum-packed), drained and
sliced
½ cup canned baby corn halved horizontally
½ cup canned straw mushrooms, sliced
8-10 string beans, cut into 2-inch pieces
½ cup green and/or red bell peppers, seeded and cut into bite-size
pieces
6 kaffir leaves

1 bunch Napa cabbage, washed and leaves separated
15 basil leaves


**Directions**

1. Combine the water, red curry paste, galangal, and rhizome in a pan or pot (optional).

2. Bring the mixture to a boil, then add the chicken and continue to cook for 10 minutes.

3. Combine the fish sauce, sugar, carrot, bamboo shoots, baby corn, straw mushrooms, string beans, bell peppers, and kaffir leaves in a mixing bowl.

4. Return to a boil, covered. Reduce the heat to low and let it simmer for 5 minutes.

5. Cook for 2 minutes longer after adding the Napa cabbage and basil leaves.

Serve with rice.


## Duck with Tamarind Sauce

serves : 2-3  people
Time to prepare: 5 minutes, plus 30 minutes marinating and 10 minutes soaking (optional)
Time to cook: 15-20 minutes

**Ingredients**
2 duck breasts, skin on, boneless
For marinade
1-star anise, toasted
2 cinnamon sticks, toasted
4 cloves garlic
1 cilantro root
1 teaspoon white pepper powder
1 tablespoon light soy sauce
1 tablespoon oil

For sauce
1 cilantro root
3 cloves garlic
1-star anise, toasted
1 teaspoon white pepper powder
1 tablespoon vegetable oil
2 cinnamon sticks, toasted
1 cup chicken stock
1 ½ tablespoon palm sugar (or muscovado, coconut, or table sugar)
1 teaspoon honey
1 teaspoon dark soy sauce
2 teaspoons light soy sauce
1 ½ teaspoons fish sauce
½ cup tamarind sauce (homemade or store-bought)
Chili paste or sauce, to taste
4 Chinese/shiitake mushrooms, rehydrated and halved (optional)
1 cup chestnuts (optional)
For steamed vegetables
Steamed baby Bok choy, bell pepper, broccoli, and baby corn (or any vegetable of choice)

For garnish
3-4 Thai chilies
Cilantro
Fried onion flakes (optional)

Directions

1. Dry the duck breasts with paper towels and make many incisions in the flesh for optimal marinade absorption.

2. Toast the cinnamon sticks and star anise for 30 seconds in a hot wok or pan.

3. Soak dried mushrooms in boiling water for 10-20 minutes before halving. Set things aside for now.

For the marinade

4. In a mortar and pestle, pound the star anise, cinnamon sticks, garlic, and cilantro to produce a coarse paste.

5. To the mixture, add the white pepper, soy sauce, and oil and massage it all over the duck breasts.

6. Cover and set aside to marinate for at least 30 minutes (the longer, the better).

7. Bake the marinated duck for 25-35 minutes at 300°F, or until the top is thoroughly browned and the meat is no longer pink.

8. Place in a serving dish.

To make the sauce

9. In a mortar and pestle, pound the cilantro, garlic, star anise, and white pepper to produce a paste.

10. Heat the oil in a wok or pan over medium heat.

11. Heat the oil and sauté the paste until aromatic.

12. Combine the cinnamon sticks, chicken stock, palm sugar, honey, soy sauces, fish sauce, tamarind sauce, and chili sauce in a large mixing bowl. Cook for approximately 1 minute, stirring occasionally.

13. Stir in the mushrooms and chestnuts (optional).

14. Continue to simmer until the sauce has thickened.

15. Taste and adjust the saltiness, sweetness, and spiciness to taste.

Remove the cinnamon sticks from the mixture and pour it over the roasted duck breasts.

16. Garnish with Thai chilies, cilantro, and fried onion flakes and serve with steamed veggies.

# MAIN DISHES WITH PORK

## Thai Lemongrass Pork Chops

4 servings
Time to prepare: 5 minutes + 2 hours marinating
Time to cook: 10-15 minutes


**Ingredients**
4 pork chops, about ¾ inch thick, rinsed and drained
Lemon zest or cilantro (for garnish)
For marinade
2 cloves garlic, minced
2 stalks of lemongrass, thinly sliced
1 teaspoon cracked black pepper
2 tablespoons brown sugar
2 tablespoons fish sauce
1 teaspoon dark sesame oil
1 tablespoon rice wine


**Directions**
1. Pat the pork chops dry using paper towels and leave them.

2. In a mortar and pestle, pound or crush the garlic, lemongrass, and black pepper. Place it in a basin.

3. Stir in the remaining marinade ingredients. Pour it on top of the pork.

4. Refrigerate the pork chops for 2 hours overnight.

5. Bring the chops to room temperature and prepare the grill to 450°F.

6. Brush the pork chops with olive oil and cook for 5-7 minutes on each side.

7. If preferred, garnish with lemon zest and serve with steamed veggies (broccoli, baby corn, Bok choy, carrot, etc.).

## Thai Pork Barbecue

4 servings
Time to prepare: 5 minutes + 15 minutes marinating
Time to cook: 15 minutes

**Ingredients**
1 pound pork tenderloin, cut into ½-inch slices
Cilantro or Thai sweet basil (for garnish)
For marinade
1 stalk fresh lemongrass, stem and coarse leaves trimmed, cut into
chunks, bruised
1 tablespoon sugar
2 tablespoons soy sauce
1 tablespoon fish sauce
1 thumb (1-inch piece) of fresh ginger, peeled and sliced
¼ teaspoon pepper
1 tablespoon Thai red curry paste
2 cloves garlic, peeled
2 tablespoons vegetable oil

**Directions**

1. Pat the meat dry using paper towels. Place aside.

2. In a blender or food processor, combine the marinade ingredients and produce a mixture, adding water if necessary.

3. Heat the grill to 450°F.

4. Marinate the pork for 15 minutes in the marinade.

5. Cook for 5-7 minutes on each side of the grill.

6. Serve with chili sauce and sticky rice garnished with cilantro or Thai sweet basil.

## Thai Tamarind Spare Ribs

4 servings
Preparation time: 1 hour and 35 minutes the day before.
Time to cook: 10 minutes

**Ingredients**

1-1 ½ pounds pork spareribs
10 kaffir lime leaves
½ cup galangal, skin scraped off and chopped
6 lemongrass stalks, bruised
10 black peppercorns
5 cilantro roots
5 cloves garlic

70

⅔ cup oyster sauce
½ cup palm sugar
5 tablespoons tamarind paste
Coriander sprigs for garnish


**Directions**

1. Place the ribs in a saucepan with enough water to cover them.

2. Combine the kaffir lime, galangal, and lemongrass in a mixing bowl.

3. Bring to a boil, then lower to low heat and continue to cook for 12 hours, or until the pork is cooked and no longer pink. Allow cooling after draining (you may preserve the stock to use in other meals).

4. In a mortar and pestle, pound or crush the peppercorns, coriander roots, and garlic to produce a paste.

5. Rub the paste all over the ribs, cover it, and place it in the refrigerator overnight to marinate.

6. When the ribs are done, take them out of the refrigerator and let them come to room temperature.

7. Combine the oyster sauce, palm sugar, and tamarind paste in a saucepan and heat to a mild boil. Reduce the heat and continue to simmer until the sauce thickens.

8. Toss the ribs in the sauce to coat.

9. Grill the ribs until they are gently browned (about 5 minutes). Another option is to cook the ribs first, then glaze them with the sauce.

10. Garnish with coriander, chile, or Sriracha sauce.

# MAIN COURSES OF BEEF

## Curry with Massaman Beef

8 servings

Preparation Time: 5 minutes, plus 40 minutes to make handmade massaman curry paste

Time to cook: 35-40 minutes

**Ingredients**

Massaman Curry Paste

3 shallots, whole and unpeeled

1 head garlic, whole and unpeeled

4-6 dried whole chilies

1 stalk lemongrass, (only lower half with stem and root) thinly sliced

½ inch piece galangal, julienned

4 pods cardamom

2 1-inch pieces cinnamon stick

5 cloves

1 tablespoon coriander

⅓ tablespoon cumin

⅓ tablespoon peppercorns

1 tablespoon salt

1 mace

1 nutmeg

1 teaspoon shrimp paste

For curry
1 ¼ pounds round or topside steak
Salt and pepper
2-3 tablespoons vegetable oil, divided
2 cloves garlic, crushed
2 ½ to 4 tablespoons massaman curry paste (homemade or store-bought), according to taste
1 (14-ounce) can of coconut milk or cream
1 cup beef stock
2 teaspoons palm sugar (or coconut or muscovado sugar)
2 large potatoes, peeled and cut into bite-sized pieces
1 large carrot, cut into chunks
2 teaspoons fish sauce, or to taste
A small handful of fresh basil leaves.
½ cup peanuts, roasted
Basil leaves (for garnish)


**Paste Instructions**

To prevent pepper burns, use rubber gloves while handling chili peppers.

1. Roast the shallots and garlic until the exterior is browned and the interior is tender over direct heat or a low flame (about 5-10 minutes).

Allow them to cool before removing the skin. Set away (you'll need them at the end of the process).

2. Remove the chilies' stems and seeds. Roughly chop the vegetables.

3. Toast the chiles and lemongrass in a wok or pan over medium heat for approximately 2 minutes, or until slightly browned and aromatic. Take them out of the skillet or wok.

4. Heat the pan and toast the other paste ingredients, EXCEPT the shrimp paste, for a few seconds.

73

5. Combine the chiles and salt in a mortar and pestle. Pound the chilies until they are roughly broken.

6. Pinch in the lemongrass. Pound in the remainder of the spices until a coarse paste is formed. This will take around 30 minutes. Although a food processor or blender may be used, pounding is claimed to extract more flavor from the components.

7. Pound in the roasted shallots and ginger to make a smooth paste.

8. Finally, pound in the shrimp paste until fully combined. The finished product should be a dark crimson, aromatic paste.

9. Place in a jar and chill. Refrigerated, it will keep for one month.


**To make curry**

Preheat the oven to 350°F.

11. Cut the steaks into 12-inch wide strips by slicing them against the grain (this kind of cut will help reduce cooking time). Season with salt and pepper to taste. Drizzle with 1 tablespoon of oil and toss to combine.

12. Melt the butter in a wok over medium-high heat. Working in batches, add 1-2 teaspoons of oil and sear and stir-fry the meat in the heated oil.

Drain the oil back into the wok with a slotted spoon while transferring the meat to an oven-safe casserole dish or Dutch oven.

13. Cook the garlic until it is aromatic (about 30 seconds). Reduce the heat.

14. Stir in the curry paste and cook for another 2 minutes.

15. Combine the coconut milk, beef stock, and sugar in a mixing bowl. Bring it to a boil, stirring constantly.

16. Stir in the potatoes, carrot, fish sauce, and a few basils leaves. Simmer for one minute.

17. Pour this mixture into the casserole dish or Dutch oven with the steak and stir thoroughly.

18. Cover and bake for 30 minutes.

Bake for 30 minutes at 375°F. The steak and potatoes should be cooked until soft.

20. Garnish with basil leaves and sprinkle with toasted peanuts.

Serve over rice.

## Beef in Yellow Curry

4 servings
Time to prepare: 5 minutes + 1 hour for homemade curry paste
Time to cook: 30 minutes

### Ingredients
Yellow curry paste
4 large shallots, whole and peeled
4 large heads of garlic, whole, outer skin removed
½ cup fresh ginger, peeled and sliced
5-20 whole dried Thai chilies
1 ½ tablespoons salt
2-3 tablespoons turmeric powder

2-3 tablespoons mild curry powder
2 teaspoons roasted ground coriander
3 tablespoons lemongrass paste
¼ cup cilantro leaves and stems, packed
For curry
⅔-1 pound beef steak, cut into thin, bite-sized pieces
1 tablespoon vegetable oil
2 ½ tablespoons yellow curry paste (homemade or store-bought), or
to taste
1 small onion, minced
1 (14-ounce) can of coconut milk
1 medium potato, peeled and cut into bite-size pieces
1 medium carrot, peeled and sliced
2 plum tomatoes, cut into wedges
2 teaspoons fish sauce
Juice of ½ lime
Cilantro, chopped (for garnish)

**Yellow curry paste preparation instructions**

To prevent pepper burns, use rubber gloves while handling chili peppers.

1. Preheat the oven to 350 degrees Fahrenheit.

2. Avoid separating the garlic cloves. Remove the sharp tips but keep the heads entire.

3. Drizzle oil over the shallots, garlic, and ginger.

4. Wrap the shallots and garlic in foil separately.

5. Layer the ginger slices in a single layer and cover them with foil.

6. Bake for 15 minutes on a baking sheet. Remove the ginger, which should be tender by now.

7. Increase the oven temperature to 400°F and roast the shallots and garlic for another 30 minutes, or until golden brown and aromatic.

In the meanwhile, soak the dried chiles in water for 15 minutes to rehydrate them. Drain.

9. Combine all of the paste ingredients in a food processor or blender and mix until smooth. In glass jars, keep refrigerated.

To make curry

10. Heat the oil in a pot or wok over medium heat.

11. Heat the curry paste in a skillet over medium-high heat until aromatic.

12. Stir in the steak and onion to coat with the curry paste.

Cook until the meat is no longer pink in the center.

13. Bring to a boil with the coconut milk.

14. Reduce the heat to low and continue to cook for 15 minutes. Tender beef is ideal.

15. Stir in the potatoes and carrots and continue to cook for another 15 minutes, or until the veggies are soft.

16. Combine the tomatoes, fish sauce, and lime juice in a mixing bowl. Remove from the heat after thoroughly stirring to mix.

17. Serve with rice and garnished with coriander.

# Curry with Beef and Peanuts

2-3 servings
Time to Prepare: 5 minutes
Time to cook: 20-30 minutes


## Ingredients
1 pound steak, cut into bite-sized pieces or strips
Salt and pepper
2-3 tablespoons peanut or vegetable oil
3 cloves garlic, minced
2 teaspoons red curry paste (or to taste)
1 small carrot, peeled and sliced thinly
1 cup potatoes, sliced
1 cup coconut milk
1 tablespoon peanut butter
½ cup red and green bell peppers (mixed), cut into bite-size
pieces
Roasted peanuts (for garnish)


## Directions
1. Pat dry the beef and season it with salt and pepper.

2. Preheat a wok or a large pan over medium-high heat. Pour
in the oil.

3. Sear the meat on all sides in the wok, then remove and put aside.

4. Sauté the garlic and curry paste in the same pan with any remaining oil (add more if required) until fragrant.

5. Stir-fry the carrots and potatoes in a pan. The color of the carrot should deepen, and the potatoes should have some brown patches. If the mixture gets too dry, add roughly 1 tablespoon of water to avoid burning. Turn down the heat.

6. Combine the coconut milk and peanut butter in a mixing bowl. Stir thoroughly and heat for 5 minutes, or until the sauce thickens.

7. Add the seared meat pieces and continue to cook until the steak and veggies are soft.

8. Add the bell peppers and cook for 1 minute more.

9. Garnish with toasted peanuts and serve with rice.

# MAIN COURSES WITH SEAFOOD

## Salmon teriyaki

Serves: 4 people
Time to Prepare: 10 minutes
Time to cook: 20 minutes


### Ingredients

4 boneless, skinless salmon fillets
2 cloves garlic, grated and pounded to a paste
1 thumb (1-inch piece) fresh root ginger, peeled and finely grated
5 tablespoon soy sauce
5 tablespoon mirin (rice wine) or dry sherry
1 tablespoon golden caster sugar
1 tablespoon sunflower oil


### Directions

1. Using paper towels, dry the salmon fillet.

2. Pound the garlic and ginger into a paste in a mortar and pestle.

3. Place the paste in a mixing dish and add the soy sauce, mirin, and sugar. Whisk to combine and dissolve the sugar.

4. Preheat a grill or a large skillet over high heat. Brush or coat the skillet with oil.

5. Lightly cover the salmon with the sauce. Bring the remaining sauce mixture to a simmer in a saucepan.

6. While the sauce is simmering, broil the salmon for 20 minutes over medium-low heat, brushing it with the sauce now and then.

Continue to cook the sauce until it is thickened and sticky.

7. Flip the fish to ensure equal cooking. When done, remove off the grill and place on a serving plate.

8. Serve the thickened sauce over the fish.

**Stir-Fry of Seafood with Basil**

4 servings
Preparation Time limit: 5 minutes
Time to cook: 8–10 minutes

**Ingredients**

1 pound mixed seafood (mussels, shrimp, scallops, calamari);
cleaned, shelled, deveined, sliced (for calamari)
3 tablespoons peanut oil
3 cloves garlic, minced
½ red and green bell pepper; cut into bite-sized pieces
½ white onion, minced
2 scallions, white part chopped; green part sliced into 1-inch long
pieces
3-4 Thai chilies, chopped
2 tablespoons oyster sauce
1 tablespoon fish sauce
1 teaspoon sugar (preferably palm sugar)
¼ teaspoon ground white pepper
¼ cup chicken stock (omit if you prefer a drier sauce)
1 cup Thai holy basil; washed, dried and stemmed

**Directions**

1. Melt the butter in a wok or pan over high heat. Swirl in the oil and heat nearly to smoking temperature.

2. Stir in the garlic for approximately 30 seconds.

3. Combine the bell pepper, white onion, white sections of the scallions, and chilies in a mixing bowl. Cook for a further 10 seconds.

4. Stir-fry the seafood until the shrimp becomes pink.

5. Bring the sauces, sugar, pepper, stock, and the green portion of the scallions to a boil in a saucepan. Cook for about 5 minutes.

6. Cook for 20 seconds, or until the basil leaves are wilted, after stirring in the basil.

7. Serve immediately with rice or noodles.

# MAIN COURSES FOR VEGETARIANS

## Stir-Fry Thai Mushrooms and Eggplant

4 servings
Time to Prepare: 5 minutes
Time to cook: 15 minutes

## Ingredients
2 pounds Japanese eggplant, cut into bite-sized pieces
3 tablespoons vegetable oil
1 tablespoon minced garlic
1 teaspoon ground chili paste
2 tablespoons minced fresh ginger
½ small yellow onion, cut into thin wedges
2 cups mixed mushrooms, sliced
½ cup carrots, julienned or spiralized
2 tablespoons soy sauce
2 tablespoons vegetarian oyster sauce or mushroom sauce
½ cup water
¼ cup fresh Thai basil leaves halved
Rice for serving

**Directions**

1. Soak the sliced eggplant in water for 10 minutes to avoid browning or darkening of the color. When ready to cook, drain and wipe dry with paper towels.

2. Melt the butter in a large wok or pan over medium heat.

3. Drizzle in the oil, followed by garlic, chili paste, and ginger.

Stir for 30 seconds, or until the mixture is aromatic.

4. Stir in the drained eggplant for 3 minutes.

5. Combine the onion, mushrooms, carrots, soy sauce, and vegetarian oyster sauce in a mixing bowl. Toss to combine.

6. Reduce the heat to low and continue to cook for 5 minutes.

7. Add the water one tablespoon at a time, stirring constantly.

8. Cook until the sauce is just thick enough to coat the back of a spoon.

9. Remove from the heat and add the basil.

10. Toss with rice


## Tofu and Steamed Mixed Vegetables

Serves: 4-6 people
Time to Prepare: 5 minutes
Time to cook: 10 minutes.


**Ingredients**
2 large broccoli crowns, cut into bite-sized pieces
1 cup green beans or string beans, topped and cut into 1 ½-
inch
pieces
2 stalks lemongrass, cut in half and bruised (optional)
1 medium carrot, peeled and sliced
½ cup mixed (red or green) bell peppers, cut into bite-sized
pieces
1 to 2 pieces Thai chili, seeded and finely chopped

84

2 scallions, cut into 1-inch long pieces
1 (8-ounce) package baked tofu, cut into bite-size pieces
Salt, to taste


**Directions**

1. In a wok or stir-fry pan, combine the broccoli florets and beans.

2. Add just enough water to keep the pan's bottom wet.

3. Scatter the lemongrass leaves on top of the veggies.

4. Cover and steam until the broccoli and beans develop a brilliant green color (about 5 minutes).

5. Combine the carrot, bell pepper, chiles, scallions, and tofu in a mixing bowl. Stir.

6. Cover and continue cooking for 3 minutes, or until all of the veggies are tender-crisp. Season with salt and pepper.

7. Serve with ricing and a peanut-coconut milk sauce on the side.


**Green Curry Vegetable Stir Fry Paste**

serves 4 people.
Time to Prepare: 30 minutes
Time to cook: 12-15 minutes

**Ingredients**
½-1 cup cashew nuts
1 ½ cup firm tofu
2 tablespoons vegetable oil
1 clove of garlic, minced
3-4 tablespoons green curry paste, or to taste
1 large onion chopped
¼ cup vegetable stock
2 cups broccoli florets
1 bell pepper, trimmed and diced roughly
1 carrot, peeled and sliced thinly
1 cup zucchini, thinly sliced
½ cup pineapple chunks
2 tablespoons oyster sauce
1 tablespoon soy sauce
½ teaspoon sugar
Cilantro leaves, to garnish (optional)

**Directions**

1. Toast the cashew nuts in an oven at 350-425° for approximately 5 minutes, spreading them on a baking sheet. Alternatively, toast them in a pan with approximately a teaspoon of oil on the stovetop.

Toss for approximately 5 minutes over medium heat. Set \saside.

2. Wrap the tofu in towels and weigh it down for approximately 30 minutes (optional, but this will make the tofu tastier). Wipe dry before cutting into 1-inch squares. Deep fry or roast in a nonstick pan (you may fry whole and do the cutting after frying).

Set the place on paper towels to drain.

3. Melt the butter in a wok over high heat. In a large skillet, heat the oil and sauté the garlic, green curry paste, and onion until aromatic.

4. Stir in the stock, veggies, pineapple, sauces, and sugar. Stir-fry the veggies until they are crisp-tender.

5. Cook for 1 minute further after adding the tofu, broccoli, zucchini, peppers, carrot, cashews, and spring onions.

6. Remove from the heat and garnish with cilantro to serve.

# DESSERTS

**Sweet Sticky Rice**

servings: 4

Preparation Time required: 10 minutes + 1 hour
Time to cook: 20 minutes.


## Ingredients
1 ½ cups uncooked Thai sticky rice
2 cups water
1 ½ cups coconut milk
1 cup white sugar
½ teaspoon salt
For sauce
½ cup coconut milk
1 tablespoon white sugar
¼ teaspoon salt
1 tablespoon tapioca starch
Accompaniment and topping
3 mangos, peeled and sliced
1 tablespoon toasted sesame seeds

**Directions**

1. Soak the sticky rice for 30 minutes to an hour in enough water to cover. Drain.

2. Place the rice in a rice cooker with 2 cups of water and set it to cook.

3. If you're manually boiling the rice, bring it to a boil, then cover and decrease the heat to low. Simmer for 15 to 20 minutes, or until the rice has absorbed all of the water.

4. While the rice is cooking, bring the coconut milk, sugar, and salt to a boil in a saucepan. Take the pan off the heat.

5. As soon as the rice is done, slowly pour in the coconut milk mixture, stirring constantly, until the rice has absorbed the sauce. You may not need to use the whole amount of sauce. Cover and set aside for 30 minutes to 1 hour, or until chilled and more pudding-like inconsistency.

6. In the meanwhile, make the sauce by combining all of the sauce ingredients in a pot. While whisking, bring it to a boil.

Set aside after removing from the heat.

7. Arrange part of the sliced mango and a cup of sticky rice on a serving plate. Pour the sauce over the top and garnish with toasted sesame seeds.

Banana Fritters

serving2-4
Time to Prepare: 5 minutes
Time to cook: 5-10 minutes

**Ingredients**
4 ripe bananas (plantain bananas are also good), peeled and sliced
lengthwise
For batter
1 cup plus 2 tablespoons rice flour
1 ½ teaspoon baking soda
½ cup sugar
1 teaspoon salt
¾ cup water
½ cup grated coconut
Oil for deep frying
For garnish/topping
2 tablespoons toasted sesame seeds, for garnish
Coconut (or flavor of choice) ice cream, optional

**Directions**
1. Sift together the rice flour, baking soda, sugar, and salt in a mixing dish.

2. Whisk in the water gradually until there are no more lumps.

3. Stir in the shredded coconut, making sure it's uniformly distributed.

4. Heat the oil in a large pan, wok, or fryer to 350°F.

5. Coat the banana slices in batter and cook until golden brown, turning a few times.

6. Pat dry with paper towels and top with toasted sesame seeds.

7. Top with scoops of coconut ice cream and serve (optional)

# CONCLUSION

The meals in this cookbook take you on a cultural journey via Thai influence on American restaurant and culinary culture. Thai flavors and spice combinations are a fantastic experience. I hope you've found your favorite Thai takeout cuisine here, and that you'll enjoy making them at home and putting your own unique twist on them. Preparing home-cooked meals for family members or even for oneself may still be a lot of fun.

**Have fun while cooking!**